axolotl waltz

axolotl waltz

Nathan Shepherdson

PUNCHER & WATTMANN

First published in 2024
Published by Puncher and Wattmann
PO Box 279
Waratah NSW 2298

https://www.puncherandwattmann.com
web@puncherandwattmann.com

ISBN   9781922571878

Cover image *Continuum 22* © Arryn Snowball, courtesy of Jan Manton Gallery
Cover design & typesetting by Morgan Arnett
Printed by Lightning Source International

NATIONAL
LIBRARY
OF AUSTRALIA

A catalogue record for this
work is available from the
National Library of Australia

time drinks rhythms misstepped in its axolotl waltz.

Giordano Pastore

Contents

3. *our feet together in hemispheres crowbarred apart*

1.

forward or backward
as our shadows slide rice grains
across a table

our heads become glass

if you turn the mirror
into a calculator
the light does not equal
your life

but this answer
is the same as the reason
why our heads become glass
when this conversation ends

because fiction can only be
the demise of truth
in the way a comma
swings through the trees of this sentence
in the same way an idea
neglects to pause at this death
just moments before
shipping containers of blood
were finally unloaded
onto an empty wharf

in the outline of a hand
torn from the first hand
is this other hand
you write with

proof of the animal
that procreates
inside forged alphabets

what we call memory
is just silence being poured
into the mould of another face
and the candied honey
they now trowel into eye sockets
is not permission for a tongue
to taste blind faith

this is your flesh
growing over a new bone
about to be broken
by the next thought

corners count a frame

so many portraits
deliberately forgotten
by their own eyes

deliberately awake
in the fact
they are not there
in their own image
because the saviour
never wrote back
because the alphabet
was still dirt
under the fingernails of a saint
disarmed into believing
lips above all
require permanence
in an oil painted kiss
where lips above all
are drawn down
as a theatre curtain
over a tooth's real intent
to be satisfied
by meat fibre at its base
or the olfactory water
sucked from half spheres
of cut passion fruit
supplied by the knife
in your lover's hand

it's not easy
to remember
that mirrors
remember us

to be reminded
how the dark-eyed Madonna
on your sloping wall
watches as much TV as you do
watches you go down on your wife
with a glass of shiraz in her hand
before all three of us
come to the same conclusion
that as portraits
time can pass over us
without breathing

and if our skin is found
stretched to the habit in a painter's hand
or if the room is found
to be undamaged by our planted gaze
we will be here
or it will be imagined we are here
when we're not / ←
→ / not even a parcel of skulls
readdressed to our impatient maker
who has no choice
but to wait for a reply
from the white stone
as comfortable as ever
in his moss-covered hand

this is as close as it gets
to the guarantee
that sleep is a fiction
and that the stones
in your father's pockets
will not sink
when he's dead

the unconsumed apple

←——————— in 1925
Oppenheimer left a poisoned apple
on his tutor's desk

only the fact was consumed

and the apple was angry
at being wasted
by two men

because an apple
would rather be eaten
than be written about

and in the investigating interview
the apple observed:

'i know that many would see me
as the core of my own problem

and yes → the symbolism is heavy
as heavy as the uranium
given the future of this man ←

but why would a man
want to exploit a piece of fruit
in such a way

i was washed by the farmer
before i was sold

and a day before
i was picked by his 12 year old daughter
her skin as unblemished as mine

i never wanted to be
a moral mechanism
polluted with the lost intent
of another brilliant mind

i am an apple

was an apple
as crisp as a snapped match
freshly broken by the fingers
from a physicist's equating hand

what good is history
when my reason for being
is obsolete

i have no value
dangerous even to an insect
and i could not be objectively viewed
even if painted into a still life

ironically red in German
will become my condition in English
here at Cambridge University.'

the apple was bagged up
and later moved off campus
to an undisclosed location

it is believed
it was destroyed in a bombing raid
in the Second World War

/ /

this apple is a periscope
to look at red in silence

the autobiography of chance

you have read the autobiography of chance

the cover is pretty tacky
with a close-up of a roulette wheel
where the numbers have been replaced by words

on the back it's more interesting
a black & white photo of Duchamp & Cage
both squeezed into a single pair of overalls
with both baring a set of dice between their teeth

it's a great photo
and in the bottom corner you can make out a blurry skull
only the right socket
so you can't tell whether it's laughing or not
but the one thing you can tell
is that both men knew how to wink from the grave

the first sentence in the book reads

the first sentence in the book reads
and when it has finished
you read the first sentence in the book
which says →
'Any resemblance to fiction is purely coincidental.'

the last sentence in the book reads

the last sentence in the book reads
and when it has finished

you read the last sentence in the book
which states →
'You must locate which part of the anatomy the head is.'

the head is

is this the head
this is the head
the head is this

now you know this

now you know this
you write the word 'this' on a slip of paper
you give 'this' and the book to a friend
who instead of reading it
tapes it to her stomach for a period of 6 months
and has templates of unfolded dice inscribed over her breasts
and you don't even have to squint to see
that this pattern is the pattern of a cross
yet despite the naff symbolism
she continues to get arrested at airports
for what she has concealed on her person

now you know this head is this
this head she has concealed on her person
this head has concealed her person
this head you now know is

and yes is

and yes is equal to all the points you carry forward ($\rightarrow$: : :)

another sentence in the book reads

another sentence in the book reads
and when it has finished
you read another sentence in the book
which advises $\rightarrow$
'Your friend is still being read by the first sentence.'

the only sentence in the book reads

the only sentence in the book reads
and when it has finished
you read the only sentence in the book
which admits $\rightarrow$
'This is the only sentence in this book.'

Oscar Niemeyer at 100
for Victoria Goring

i draw a coffin
in the shape of my head

i want you to build this
as a giant memory
overlooking the sea

the engineer slaps his forehead
decrying that it can't be done

i open my hands out towards him
as if to catch his assertion

but you see : : : : : →
people are already living there

and your skill
should be to grow a structure around them
without disturbing their habits

50 years ago i won the argument
by convincing weight to leave concrete
by pouring concrete from my mind

i simply persuaded space
to rupture different ideas
with different locations

James Stirling is pulled into a flat line

for Michael Keniger

i leave my body
on the operating table
to go for a coffee
with the anaesthetist

. i never return .

the anaesthetist ←
somehow removed his eyes
with the point of return
spread my pain too thin
opting for axonometric treatment
over traditional perspective

iodine bloom to orange
protracts my skin
as a horizontal wall →

the language of the house
tells me there is a hernia
in the floorboards

propeller/Le Corbusier

for Rebecca Hoffman and Grant Buglar

as the propeller
slices the thigh
of his swimming form/

Le Corbusier is reminded
that machines are not just
for living in
but for dying
under as well

he might surface
in the wash
of a boat's violent remark

holding together
with blood irony
how his leg can be
undesigned

he realises buildings
should not be
photographed
until flesh
has fallen
off their bones

a white shirt is

a white shirt
wind sings its hymn
to torso empty absence
absence still
dreams the collar into white lips
unspoken
dissolved through emptier tongue
it dissolves into absence
as unflesh reabsent

as absence is a planet is
we never see
until we are
where it is
a planet is
with or without sleeves
white as one held breath
it will finally not knock
at the door it will not open
until it is not the space
it does not occupy
can not be worn as the shirt
it is

it was
as cloth rumoured should be
forgotten not to be begging
at altitude from our eyes made
bleached azalea white
our eyes could this shirt fold

against its will
tourniqueted around light its own
restrict to the bodyknot
birth with no memory no
form into fact and vanishing
is into into is
is into is

is a shirt
not an actor to become
at any stage
of its existence
is not an actor
if it exists
it exists if
if it exists
is not a shirt

is this and
is this and
this and is the woman is
who air removed from shirt
who breathed did no life
air in whom air is soaked
into the lisp in transparent
soaked from shirt beneath
blood two spots
were his nipples were once
two bloods grow
once she eyes closes
once burning the shirt is

the 3 point plan for post-modern decision making in the year 2006

for Kathryn Roberts

inappropriation (1.)

yes →
we know
that everything could be something else
but it could also be nothing
which is the reason
we should write about it
because if we didn't
then we'd have to say something wouldn't we
and if we did that
then what would we talk about
maybe we should stop thinking about this
so we can start → O
thinking about something else
maybe we should forget
what we have just said
so we can talk about nothing
that way
we can think of the best way
not to say what we want to say
and end up trying to speak
with a mouth full of silence

unappropriation (2.)

yes →
we know
that anything could be everything else
but it could also be something
which is the reason
we shouldn't write about it
because if we did
then we'd have to say nothing wouldn't we
and if we did that
then what would we talk about
maybe we should start thinking about this
so we can stop → ⊙
thinking about something else
maybe we shouldn't forget
what we have just said
so we can talk about nothing
that way
we can think of the best way
to say what we won't say
and end up trying to speak
with a mouthful of silence

nonappropriation (3.)

yes ←
we did not know
that something could be everything else
but it could also be anything
which is not the reason
we should not write about it
because if we did
then we'd have to say everything wouldn't we
and if we did that
then what would we talk about
maybe we should deny thinking about this
so we can pretend → ◎
we're thinking about something else
maybe we shall forget
what we have just said
so we can talk about nothing
that way
we can think of the best way
not to say what we will say
and end up trying to speak
with a mouthful of silence

underline a number
for David Mahon

(→somehow←)
we inherit the distance between planets
using our birth date as a ruler
to underline a number
once counted
is almost gone

breathing elects us
to this common principle
on the understanding
that our bones
will be shaved back
to a fact

you will be given one word
to gently blow across the page
tilt it in the air
like dried skin from an acrobat
rehearsed into an absent body
a flesh diagram inhaled by its outline
as the page is kept mobile
pinched between thumb & forefinger
in both hands is the incomplete dance
that sways the white square
into the illusion
that unlanded light
can make itself into an eye
but instead allows you to see

how as a hunter
you are trapped
in your necessary pursuit

without malady
you consult the doctor
who explains how external space
can elastically expand as internal space
when placed inside something
that is outside of itself
and to illustrate
he puts his hand inside your dimensional pocket
and shows you the rolled lint
you quickly perceive will be your past
because every time you blink
another door opens somewhere
onto its own description
which enables you to walk through it
by standing still

as you leave
the doctor hands you a script
cryptically written in petrarchan form
and he tells you
'this is the pattern
best sung in four parts'
because he knows
if you 'apply this pattern to the music
that will float your ears to their surface'
it will have more significance
than any other

. . .

hopefully you remember
the two young men
in a small blue car
driving past the mountain
proof to the sculptural genius
of geology sitting beside the science
is the myth as clear as a road sign
demanding they slow down
to give due respect to impermanence
while the future accelerates around them
as they continue to stare at the mountain
as the mountain stares out to sea
while the small blue car
amounts to a comment in a bitumen margin

. . .

tomorrow morning
both men will wake up
in their respective houses
to find they are each
inside a pen
on a table

poem for non-interpretation

for Joe Daws

this is a portrait of this idea
in its belief
it cannot believe
it is something else

other than a conversation
smudged up to a surface
without words still there
on the shopping list
of a well closed eye
not looking to buy time
until its lungs too
are empty emptied enough
to be called space

how precise it all is
when it is not known

as it happens
in this circumstance
observation is interference
caught in the left hand
covered in kid seams
once stitched into definition
by what was known
as a 'dream'

(   ) a word that still bathes
in our greyest blood
a word on which
the 20th century wiped its feet
until the holes resembled birth canals
for theory (   )

it's just as easy
to wipe your own feet
at your own door
and have yourself open it
from the inside
before you can knock

and now we talk about objects
as if they're real

take one step forward
to remove yourself from the abstraction
into the abstract

take one step back
to place yourself at your birth
where you stand as an old man
holding your mother's hand

read this aloud to no one

do not read this aloud
to anyone

(least of all yourself)

explaining pictures to a dead hare
for Isaak Shepherdson

even before modernism
Turner used to mop up the sky with a bread roll

and famously Dürer
convinced your breathing precursor
to sit as still as this word ←
some 500 years ago

even – now
your physically rearranged brothers & sisters
with blood abandoned by tyre squeegees
on the satisfied white arrows of a highway
are still ←
contributing to what we know as ART

we can only hold these eyes in our head
so they can't see themselves

we can only occupy an image
once it's been evacuated

where once we are
we're once

where once the artist interrogated form
now form interrogates the artist

we are moving towards the day

when people will not wince
when shown a heart diced on a plate

and i sense you're wondering
how to digest all this irony

you would do well to remember
that although the half-smirk
is an acknowledged critical apparatus
it is also part entrance
unconsciously led to the intestine

if we look at this picture over here →
you can see the intricate way
theory has been combed over its surface
to a point
where the artist ends
as a fringe taped to his own mirror

theory has a right
to imagine itself
tripping over mountains

i am not suggesting
that i know what i'm talking about
anymore than i know
what you're thinking

but i am suggesting
that i might find an idea
worthy of standing in front of
for as many years as it takes

to seduce myself into your equal state

as (it) happens
i would not recommend those heads

endlessly wrapped in endless images
(their thoughts) unlikely to germinate

any or all forms of geometry
recognisable or not
need to eat through their own corners
in order to survive

the abstract is simply fishing for our minds

this allows us to be here when we're there

light is our possessor
and light accuses us
in a way that says
it is also time

this is why ←
we should close our eyes
and admit that what we want
is to see a pod falling
sodden with inhaled notions
to burst at our feet
in entire dark

understanding is also a politics

and any form of politics
needs to be fumigated with silence
before it can be considered

perhaps history (is) easier to find than the thing

and this history ←
seems a bank account
for the sole deposit of bones

i can't tell if you've noticed
how i covered my head in gold paint
burnishing a little on your forehead as well
because i want us connected
and i want to introduce the suspicion
that our heads are the same frames
that a century ago would've been on the wall

something else →
made from another whisper
continues to climb down from my ear
then slide into yours

your body is the weight of my absence

and i know one day ←
you will burrow home in my sleeve
and i will be covered in your fur

○

your failure to answer will defeat this sentence.

————wrotisserie————

————————————sing this until death listens————————————

————————you have the lung capacity of two commas————————

————————i arrive at your ears before the thunder————————

————clouds are not thoughts but should not be clouds————

————————only one of our lives will be believed————————

————————we are too old to penetrate this decision————————

————————you offer the chair a place to stand————————

————————i am surplus to my needs————————

————————this piece of string crawls towards scissors————————

————————this piece of fruit befriends probability————————

———————————you omit the finger to admit the hand———————————

———————————the plural singles itself out———————————

———————————what is sudden asks our patience———————————

———————————this is the tree that will cut us down———————————

———————————a wound unconvinced that it is fatal———————————

———————————a cup unforeseen at the lips of your mirror———————————

———————————we admonish the square for its rectitude———————————

———————————our arms too inaccurate to throw light into corners———————————

———————————we hang space on the nail we nail into space———————————

———————————sleep & distance announce their engagement———————————

————————on one anniversary no one remembers————————

————————to behead the cliché time rolls its last cigarette————————

————————i embarrass fate by denying it————————

————————we borrow the animal from its maker————————

————————in the dream the urine the urine can't detect————————

————————i offer insight to a bag of rust————————

————lengthening the queue at the pharmacy to purchase regret————

————————our skin made of undeliverable conclusions————————

————the sociology we invest in one magnet to usurp two brains————

————————these transplants we practice with wicker hearts————————

————————giving birth to carnivals between our toes————

————your name just as good as a shovel for burying memory————

————————we spit at ghosts inside this nude diamond————

————————you lick the stone to appease the stone————————

—you persist in putting ands between things that are not together—

————do you think we should tell the idea that it is there————

—we have a cannon powerful enough to shoot dogs at the moon—

————————history slept in this morning————————

————and this is a sky pulled out from under its falling————

——blue without colour the simplest colour to demonstrate blue——

————we are captions on outmoded forms of behaviour————

————we poke the sun with a stick to annoy it————

————what we're after is what we're before————

————i teach you to memorise wealth————

————i know how much i resemble this sentence————

————it is our voices that herd these words————

—these inrageous proportions that force silence to mine its mine—

————sometimes our bones are needed to make a loom————

-sometimes we can't be bothered answering the door to the disease-

————as expected we've had our tongues cut into keys————

————we put lipstick on a bell to make it sound beautiful————

————a ladder is placed up against a candle for aging moths————

————————this fog replenished with streetlights————————

————————our ancestral prayers still in packets————————

————i am paid to guard this incubator full of zeroes————

————————what do you mean by 'syllabus of hope'————————

————draw a circle on your bed and ask your life to land on it————

————————our legs to be broken in our favourite places————

————i've never noticed the tiny stairwell on your neck before————

————these emphatic shoes that walk me to your opinion————

————————the crease in the map that leads to our grave————————

————————which side to part the hair on your absence————————

——nothing i'd rather be then nothing i'd rather be then nothing——

——nothing but praise to disown the unity of our assumptions——

————————a brick either solid or violent————————

—windows love to share the joke about 'the blind leading the blind'—

————————we are just part of this extended family of intent————————

————————it took years to sail this boat to the corner of your eye————————

————————what separates the line is what joins the line————————

————————what do you mean by 'existence is a symptom'————————

————this hasty turpentine smiled into a bowl of water————

————originally you wore bodily our species initials as a prank————

————this time i'll send the mistake back to be made properly————

————you seem anxious to end this day without breathing————

————i can model your whole memory in one night————

————we will stay together until we are fiction————

————there are full stops stored in the ovaries of your shadow————

————will you arrest me if i kill you————

————i'd be lying if i was telling the truth————

————you are the only part of only i don't understand————

|2.

to the side of the womb
where your silt hand
covers the switch

the trawler

for Alun Leach-Jones

a common parliament of seagulls
ensures a consistent level of demand and abuse
as the catch hits the trawler deck
fresh human heads flop in panic
bright colours amass as pointillist glints
some scales around the eyes so gold
you'd swear they were bounty
off hands unshaken for centuries

the gills a recent evolutionary curiosity
composed slits starting behind the ear
and following the line of the jaw
now out of water
flare with asthmatic inefficiency

the tails an eonic transformation of hair
a glutinous~muscle~keratin~coat
tapered with eel ingenuity from scalpback
now physically protest their depleted energy
to indifferent splinters on the killing floor
aware that in non-liquid space
function might as well be a wreath

we need to remind our fishmonger selves
that there is no profit in admiration
and if all echoes are removed from any scenario
we will hear what we are supposed to hear
that hard work is the best Christian answer . . .

the first heads we throw back are the politicians
opposite to romantic suicides but just as poisonous
celebrity heads look good but are tasteless
scientific heads taste great but might kill you
the heads of our own families are out of the question
and military heads might explode on the first bite
musical heads are fine but can repeat on you
the heads of poets though reputedly excellent to eat
are alas tossed away because of low market value
the prize heads are philosophers and artists
the filleted cheeks a noted delicacy
the white flesh lean and stained with mistakes
it flakes like succulent talc
a moist thread from the tongue to St Peter's table

✖

for 25 years you've lived in a tank on my desk
and despite habitat taunts to both of us
you remain happy
not just because i spared your life
but because our intellect locks two elements
and dispenses molecules as a means of affection
and when i need to clean your water
i briefly hold you in my hands
and still marvel how each scale is a mirror
in this interlaced blue wrinkle-free foil
even thoughts are reflected
in the fact that i've never seen another since
the world fell into the ocean
and you returned to the surface
knowing the human line of thousands of rewound lives

i've had many offers from emporia
their saliva behind dam walls made of knives
their washed plates as ready as sin
but there is no temptation
because my impotence in all this
creates your strength to exist
your blood colder than mine and more perfect
age has refused to tie you to any clock
and one day my bones will become ornaments
on the gravel beneath your fins

if anything
we allow a skerrick of authentic fantasy
'a skerrick'- in such a word
the second r can be turned backwards
to form a bridge
with a small but unbreachable gap
where we suspend
and are suspended
in each other's minds

but for now all we can do
is imagine our different paths to oxygen
while i continue to feed you krill and commas

our gourami glass kiss
as important as the glazier's phone number

notes taken by a doll in Vienna

AM/OK

this is not a metaphor ←

this is pure illustration →

feeding his intestine
onto a spinning wheel
to form a thread
to ensure their distance stays
(connected)

their eyes too stay
(connected)
preserved with unassailable affection

●

with the thread spun
their separate parcels of breath
are placed on the scales

no child is to be weighed

OK/AM

death is an unreliable commentator.

we resist conversation with autobiography.

whether a mirror
can reform around our outline
tells us if we are caricature
or a portrait

we are not caricature ←

our heads in natural proportion
with our raptor forms
coalesced on a ledge
talon on talon
our mouths unkissing clamps
as we pinch either end of our snake
looped in graphic demise
as much as intimacy can dictate
our improbable myth to silence

●

when silent →

we fly
through the hole
in the moon

the itch

for Hamish Sewell

having stuffed the chicken
with the pages of a Russian novel
i realise i've used the wrong chapter

perhaps i should admit
i never read it
in the first place
second time around
i won't read it either
because the wine is open
the oven's at the correct temperature
and the guests are at the door

as the proverb says . . .
'the itch
won't fail the thought
calling for help
under the skin'

start two names with one syllable
i.m. Val Vallis 1916 – 2009

this (is) the right time
to turn bones into words

to forgive the fact
before the fact is knowledge
while the fact is knowledge
i cannot forgive
not knowing who to forgive
or why i am forgiven

point (to) the lapse
wherein is is wherein
in this lapse
is the static certainty
we retrieve from ourselves
to reward ourselves
as our own pets

and when asked
asked when to explain
the 12 year old will say
'you just put pencils
between your toes
and keep walking
until you realise
the lines are blood
not drawn . . .
but there all the time
beneath your feet . . .'

and when it's over
you have your skull
made into a lamp
so you can see
where your eyes should be
rather than where they are
without being we are
as we should be . . .
an unowned lamp
never wholly turned on
always under threat
of being
turned off
of off of off
as it pretends its absence
with a polite flicker
every time a word is born
or dies
slightly dims
whenever a word
never makes it
to the page at all . . .

but at 92
a man simply dissolves
his face
dusted over a clock
his memory
tests the holding capacity of air
just for a moment
his life
could've been dragged up
in one of his own nets

but we'd hidden the sea
from his view

his distance returns
his distance returns
his distance returns
without him

neck

if he replaces his neck
with another arm
it gives him more options . . .

he could make his head
into a shot put
polish a smirk
and threaten lightly
to throw it
in a new record breaking attempt

or

he could simply place his head
on a silver tray
utilising his 3rd elbow
and his 3rd wrist
to offer it waist high
as a ripe canister of thought
to the best of her intentions

new life

for Davida Allen

into the smallest hand
can be traced
all knowledge we own
with a single finger
clockwise (in the circle)
we arrive at where we start
again inside the illusion
we see is not an illusion
after all we are here
able to see each other
despite the absence of mirrors
we know are there
to simply be looked at
while the future looks at us
and seeing us in its own form
demands that we (still clockwise)
trade time for love as blood
under the surface of memory
as ourselves under the surface
of ourselves as the surface
is memory traded in mind
to approximate the place
we recognise as each other
understood into gravity
we become the eyes
let fall onto new life
and what sound is pink
or any colour (not clockwise)

that can even begin as sky
of leaf held in imagining
itself as a green hand
noticed by wind
producing movement
in other shadows
unable to produce
its own shadow
it still breathes into eyes
planted blue
deep in a child's face
reflected is a giant tree
(a hoop pine)
an example of eaten light
it could easily exaggerate
its vertical place in the world
but instead
stands still in a painting
unable to escape
the perpetual nose of a black dog
on the scent of 3 generations
its 4 legs (perhaps anti-clockwise)
avoid a straight line
around a well marked trunk
it continues to sniff and rewind
its steps to a family
in its present landscape
in its distance a house
'the doorstop of our being'
that frames our sleep
every night we should watch
the baby dormantly dressed

in its soft skull a design
a twitch as muscles as strings
pull instinct to determine
to temperature set the body

of this ember with limbs
we walk (without clock or leaving)
into another thought inherited
direct red
under a closed eyelid in full sun
we our hearts quarry
emerge at end of day
with images safe as prayers
the small hand
now joined delicate with its other
in unwilted silence
we say nothing but agree
skin is our original manuscript

corduroy linesman

for pascAlle ginsbürt

when i was six years old
my mother made a corduroy cover
for my tongue / got me
to stand in front of the mirror
and repeat the word 'manage'
until saliva had fully impregnated
its cloth ribs

importantly the corduroy was navy blue.

elected king
a fresh stick of charcoal
proposes its use from my bedside table
each morning / i am forced
to draw around my rare foot
onto a white floor
to prove who i am

importantly the charcoal is heart black.

who is i was
briefly inside a photographer
briefly inside my name
i ride the pony / through a biopic
that was an accurate quotation
from the only person in the world
who does not have my name

importantly his name is not mail box red.

the stones are turning
i.m. Bernice McCabe 1920 – 2006

what if Rodin's Thinker just stood up
put on a smart suit
walked into the next century
got a job as a government actuary
started work on every likelihood
started to collect every thought
to cram it all → to compress it all
between the binary bookends of 1 & 0?

then that delicious polished lichen patina
would move upwards from that famous fist
that unpunishing fist
over the chin over the lips
split its flow either side of the nose
creep over hair palings over the lower eyelids
suction its journey to the eyeballs' backs
and settle as a bronze answer on the brain.

this is simply thinking.

from the brain
to the brain
to the brain
from the brain

this is simply thinking.

we are decided by science
what can be → could be drawn in chalk
can be → could be found in space
in the smallest space the widest consequence
in the alloy the theory
in the mind the thought not thought
in the statement the necessity of the statement
we imagine we're somewhere else to be here.

therefore → tip the dye into the data
watch the currents appear in your abstract flesh
as at a cup my life-blood seemed to sip
remake the statue unmade into the man
unmake this fossil into this animal
the stones are turning in graves made for their birth
different leaves are about to fall onto the same ground
therefore → glue the fact to the promise.

a) in the parallel in the parallel lines in intelligence.
b) bend an atom into a future.
c) the clocks on our shoes open their eyes when we walk.

fern heads

there is one day a year
when his collar bones soften
and curl like fern-heads
forming ornamental nodes
on each shoulder

& today from the left node
he hooks his ever-lengthening ladder
woven over decades from catgut strings
and just before it brushes the ground
a hole opens next to his feet
the ladder a continued gravity
into an invitation
into a blind parallel

he climbs down from himself
sometimes for minutes
sometimes for months
the risk to predict
when the when is when
his collar bones will regress
to true anatomy

he passes captions/phrases
words suspended in the graffiti
from previous descents

everything has changed
because he left it
the way it was

memory now self-propagates
no longer requiring a brain
to form or forget

this time ↔ this time

he finds a pair of hands in prayer
lying on their side
half buried in words
riddled with electrolysis

(⊥)

he picks them up
heavier than the answers they never received
he starts his reascent to the surface
but with every rung
the hands double in weight
is what at ↔ at what is
perhaps the midpoint
he is forced to let them go
in a rubber-pulse moment
in a dust-hard punch to earth
the thud triggers a full body outline
to grow from the wrists

quickly coloured in with flesh
her first new breath complete

she opens her eyes
and sees him on his ladder

and he sees himself
as a teenage girl

runner in a landscape of dead poetry

for Gordon Shepherdson

count the inventions of sound
then put them back into silence
the murdered still murder the stillness
break their fingers in absent windows
still shape what is still with what is still
a head cuts its orbit
removes into a space twice removed
with what is still still shape what is still
what is still still shaped with what
the legs sing into the ground
displace the machines in shadows
shadows breathing blind light
cellular black minced with form
shadow a breath into a shadow
the running falls out of the bones
the bones emptied out of the shadows
these shadows were once these bones
emptied from what is now full but dissolved
what is still is still dissolved
in a dissolving frame a head cuts its orbit
cuts its throat
stops breathing as the thought begins
begins to become a shadow without a head
without wings this head will fall
unconnected into disconnected time
unconnected onto disconnected surfaces
this head will fall
fall through gaps in spacious flesh

this head will fall
alone it casts its shadow
casts its net into a sea of eyes
casts its frame into an immobile world
unfound and unlost
roughly painted with saliva
sponged off this head falling head
half fallen as if
half fallen as if
half fallen as if
the sound of wings
was only the sound of wings
the sound of wings
was only the sound
was the only sound
capable of being still
still running still
blood / spume
sand / heart
tide marks on a mirror
speed / reflection
still running still
he chases the unchaste head
replaces the machine in the shadow
the suture marks on the mirror
the suture marks on a map
replaces the machine in a mirror
replaces the map with a shadow
still running still
through walls
through doors
through sunsets

but not through memory
not through time and not through words
unfound and unlost
unable to invent skin
he invented the sound of a full stop falling
falling half fallen into an upturned head
he runs across frozen pages
carries dead words to dead thoughts to dead history
to something other than itself
to something other than a question
to something other than ego
a vein cannot decide which way it flows
blood and ideas mixed to a paste
wiped over the thighs
the feet knit the ground with motion
sugar is added to lead then swallowed
swallowed again by the falling head
the falling head
further still from its orbit
further still still further from murdered stillness
the invited guest in the gravity palace
he cut off his wings to stain the air
weighed the shadows before the light could dry
became the transcript of falling as he fell
hit the ground running
running past buildings made of ears
running past barometric souls behind glass
running past domes of sleep
the weather dead at the feet of prediction

/ SPLICE /

(40 lines i wish i'd written from films i wish i'd seen)

1

/ you are watching artifice murmur to an object /

2

/ the chair you are sitting on would make a more reliable witness /

3

/ so hold a gun to my head and tell me Godot is here /

4

/ i can tell by the rust on your lips that you haven't lied for weeks /

5

/ i love it when we swap hands in the dark
then pretend we're both alone /

6

/ let's pour our lives into each other's mouths
count to 3 and swallow /

7

/ let's staple faith to our favourite guide dog and get out of here /

8

/ you drive the car and i'll build the road /

9

/ his eyelids became transparent as he thought about you /

10

/ the rain was singing through your teeth /

11

/ she had already put in her application to
become the sense of smell /

12

/ she placed two lanceolate leaves over his eyes
and told him to wait until autumn /

13

/ if you force the stars through a sieve
light suddenly becomes edible /

14

/ in a sugar cube the size of a spare bedroom Krzysztof sleeps /

15

/ it's not unusual for memories in scuba gear to
climb out of a well made coffee /

16

/ by chance they turned our heads into dice and
threw us across the table /

17

/ we put in a window where our life used to be /

18

/ you put rumours in cages and convinced your friends to feed them /

19

/ i'm sick of dragging your big grey heart around in this rickshaw /

20

/ as i crawl on graphite limbs on a white floor to the foot of your bed /

21

/ treat the sun like a bitch and make it shine /

22

/ go and pull Artaud out of his bath with the hooks on your tongue /

23

/ she thought about carbonating his blood and drinking it with ice /

24

/ the entrails left over from the sin are the most delicious part /

25

/ i once had a job changing the light bulbs in
Francis Bacon's paintings /

26

/ the safest place i could be right now would be inside your lungs /

27

/ don't answer this question until i'm far enough away
to be the answer /

28

/ so i began my address to this crowd of anonymous people dressed
in their fly screen suits /

29

/ through a slit in the door as you undressed i saw the black &
yellow stripes on your torso /

30

/ although beautifully polished Kafka's shoes could not evade
movement or stillness /

31

/ weren't you the first man to take out a restraining order
against his shadow /

32

/ you could pierce the Devil's nipples with those eyes /

33

/ how can you just put handles on your victims and
carry them around like that /

34

/ i had to walk away with only the loose change from
redemption in my pocket /

35

/ keep the truth under the foreskin of a dead man and
freeze it for the second coming /

36

/ i am about to tell you what Eve really said to Adam /

37

/ the train said very little before it hit me /

38

/ they found the wings → then 300 metres further
→ the body of an angel /

39

/ he asked that his arms be at 45° so that rigor mortis
would make him into an arrow /

40

/ now that we're in control which half of the world do you want /

3.

our feet
together in hemispheres
crowbarred apart

when we should remember what is not said

she cleans her fingernails with a question mark

leans across her unfinished breakfast and says
'you know when we get there
we won't know where we are'

my reply isn't great but makes it through customs
'but this is why we're here
to separate chance from our outcomes'

of course
we are just persuading ourselves
that we are not as clever by halves
that went in search of the whole
and never returned

and we won't find
the skeletons of spoons
submerged in cups of tea

the news tells us
that execution has become a hobby

we spread the sun onto our toast
and talk to each other
about what we'll do today

yesterday was as our answering machine predicted
'you are yet to find the neutrality
of obsolete desire'

we test the strength of our lips
by the number of words
they can break in a day

we choose a colour scheme
that can draw the scent of the moon
through an open window

we grade the heart
by the size of the hole
it leaves in the table

the absolute intelligence
of this white flower
talking to its vase

the moment
promoted and murdered
by its own lenient version of beauty

we think about a life
the flavour of logic
with its excess
obeying the face of a knife
and then we breathe
in the direction of habit
thanking meditations under stones
for their polite consideration

language is sudden ends repaired with words

she tosses me a new carbon full stop
along with a shaved comment
'here → put this at the end of your poem' .

William & Catherine

either side of their table
William & Catherine Blake
are shelling commas

an intricate task
each one is nested in the soft v
formed with the two index fingers
the comma rested face down
under pressure from living brackets
the topographical edges of their thumbnails
meeting at their waists
to shape an efficient tool

the husk is separated from the kernel

the husks are set aside but not wasted
will be ground down to a binding agent
for use in ink in William's prints
a secret ingredient milked black
through ducts submerged in millboard catacombs
lost cold inside profound speech

& William & Catherine
regularly glance up at each other
happy that their industry
can produce the invisible sinkers
needed to weigh down the smiles
they throw in front of each other

the kernel is separated from the husk

the kernels as they usually are
are set aside in the slipware dish
depicting the 'Pelican in her Piety'
with letters brushed and bled under the glaze
the Congreve fragment
feed thee out of my own vitals

and when the quantity says so
William & Catherine unstop a homemade ale
pour it with care into a pair of tankards
as if to manufacture scales for conversation
to discuss what's wrong with The World
and to rearrange Art & Poetry as they should be

fresh commas are an aphrodisiac

and in the most intense moments
William sees words emerge on Catherine's lips
wiping them backwards on a spare page
from right to left for tomorrow's poem
to write backwards to look forwards
to spread the double landscape over their bodies
to open it wide into another prophetic book
as it lays astride the valleyskin on Catherine's chest
with Death on the left and God on the right
with their own spines two parts of the clamp
that can permit and halt this soulscythe perception

and at the end
they come upon the half grain of sand
that is more than enough
to clog a giant mind

there is no rest for the wicked
because the wicked are unable to see
where the rests were removed from their sentence

, ,

it took as many commas
to fill an unintended moon
as it did to build a lone thought

i cannot be here
for Ariel Shepherdson

i cannot be here until i leave

his continued presence
has caused the top line
of this equals sign
to bow

to a point
where the bottom line
of this equals sign
no longer believes
in the parallel virtue
or for that matter
this matter that once was
two philosophical crossbeams
safe in permanent separation

and the last time
an equals sign collapsed
the writing hands of mathematicians
were offered instead of answers
blood overflowing from
blood overflowing from
the mutual selves in equation

certainty was in fact
certainty was in fact
only just saved from drowning

in its own blood its own equation
to make sure its own blood
could be properly drowned
in its own certainty

his continued presence
continues to bend
continues the top line
of this equals sign

regardless then
then regardless
whether this equals sign
collapses or not
a core sample
should be taken
from the silence
between these two lines

and his name
will not be heard

because it is there

ten acres of silence

you sold me
ten acres of silence
telling me
i could plant our thoughts
in rows that match
these potato-stamp lines
on our foreheads . . .

weeks later
i am not surprised
to find the fruit
are vertical replicas
of your uninjected lips
capped in lace chlorophyll
and inside each
is a saliva capsule
containing what will be
on another day
two red commas . . .

the taste
wires me instantly to the day
we took a complimentary butcher's calendar
off your mother's kitchen wall
and put white sugar mounds
on our respective birth dates
swapped chairs
closed our eyes
and trying not to laugh
with our tongues hanging

impersonating new drooling limbs
we move as slowly as possible
towards what we know
^ is there ^

words coat the object

↓ the venom prays to its simplicity as it kills you

    sets clouds loose under your softening fingernails

    producing the type of smile drawn on a tree with a knife

    you have more than one enemy

    and i am more than one of them

↓ sleep is damaged at this altitude

    all commas are hammered flat for use in acupuncture

    the vertebrae protrude like questions on your back

    i walk my fingers one either side of your spine

    stop at the point on the neck most likely to break

↓ the roof answers the rain

    countless decisions fall in places other than memory

    your body floating to the surface of your white dress

    eyes leak through your skin as i move towards you

    you have swallowed my head with one word

↓ words coat the object

you untie its outline and feed it into raw space

you index my anatomy with the same science

keep my tongue on a shelf in your library

it says i was not with you when we disappeared

↓ cremated echoes are an uncommon freight

newly embossed onto the lips of your inner ear

they are extruded as spokes into the whispering wheel

listening was too hard for your soft voice

you transformed my deaf face into a stain

↓ you are in this thought because you had nowhere else to go

for some reason i agreed to plagiarise your existence

with simple carpentry you turned my chest into a bed

arranged twelve eggs in the pattern of a still clock

in this instant we stop evolution and repair our shadows

↓ you attach a signal to a wire to illuminate your name

   harden its spelling with the black polymers in your breath

   this line incised and served through our forms by the draper

   our old friend who placed us side by side in his window

   encouraged us to comb the arrows out of each other's hair

↓ i have patented the contents in your mirror

   my image of your image cannot be reproduced

   we have slowed the light enough to put it on a leash

   our paralysis is in itself a sin

   when we sigh we're guilty of murder

↓

unlike

unlike the trick that never works

you can pull the page out
from under its words
without disturbing even a comma

then you hold the page up to your face
breathe all over its surrendered white
with ample cold morning condensation

and with the paper as moist as your intent
you firmly smooth it back over its words
replanting their meaning in their reverse view

the mirror asks if it can read it
so you hold the page up to another face
check the passage for slippage with a half closed eye

it is not possible
to force any page
to read too much into itself

it is possible
to set this printed silence on fire
and put yourself out with its smoke

↑
↓

but this would involve a whole other trick

one that equips each thought
with a fire extinguisher to douse the pilot lights
in unwanted memory

↕

we've been asleep long enough

two brackets in the same bed

a full stop reaches the end of its sentence

a full stop
never understands
the need to understand
what words are for

a full stop
feels it is superior
because it provides
meaning without letters

a full stop
does understand
its capacity to arouse
a body into silence

(into silence
into silence
into silence
walks a sleeping figure
a sleeping figure
with her necklace of full stops)

for obvious reasons a full stop's favourite letter is i

a full stop has no desire to transgress its shape
a full stop is a self-incubating form
a full stop will float in water but not in blood

memories are in fact a transfusion of full stops

(full stops
have now replaced
have now replaced
are still replacing
still replacing
the sand
in the hourglass)

full stops colonise the reverse side of the mirror
full stops plot the continued downfall of words

full stops
can smell the lips of shadows
through a closed book

full stops
can be worked like fillings
into the teeth of language

full stops are sometimes set on fire
and dropped from a great height
onto the bare skin of an ending

on the odd occasion
a poet is blinded
when a full stop explodes

in an emergency
full stops can be made
by slicing the ears from commas
these will not have the same longevity
as ones naturally conceived

there was a king
who kept full stops under his foreskin
he felt they were sentinels
able to repel impotent likelihoods
as an old man
he had them set into a ring for his heir

centuries ago full stops traded their voices for stillness
full stops have happily held themselves hostage ever since

for those with the skills and the inclination
larger full stops can be filleted on a table
then added as seasoning to a cooked up theory

full stops are qualified to operate
the elevator in the spinal cord
full stops monitor all movements
between moment and sensation

full stops will migrate an immense distance to pursue conclusion

a full stop can kill an ego without moving

a handful of full stops cannot be lifted

full stops clog the pores in the face of an unwilling god

most full stops believe their god to be an eclipse
most full stops do not have a mother

full stops with imperfections
are sent to work for question marks

flies are attracted to full stops
when they are in flower

lies are the only natural predator of the full stop

one full stop equals the circumference of one thought

a full stop alone can hear gravity's song
its black yolk heavy with philosophical protein

placed in the tear ducts at the point of death
one pair of full stops will absorb the entire memory

he could never bring himself to use full stops that were still alive
he would suck them back off the page through a glass straw

full stops are very superstitious about their placement

a full stop
will gladly dissolve
its own parliament
in its own mind

(a blank page
actually a
cemetery
white with
white with
white with
bleached
bodies
the bleached bodies
of crumbling full stops)

aposiopesis

in different rooms Walser * & Wölfli **   use thoughts instead of furniture ‡

1.

i have come to regret that i understand what doors say

windows on the other hand never want to talk to me

when they invent 'yes' i will be hidden from its meaning

these predators are asleep now

when they wake they force me to put me in their sentence

after so many years it is no longer a challenge to bead silence

2.

in this world i am the painted egg that orbits around me

i put a lid on top of the world to stop it from going stale

once i would've unlocked their faces with violence

i draw as loudly as a line can

to warm myself i make pelts out of their habits

i won't believe you unless you say 'i won't believe you'

when i am alone i am not made of apologies

i trap possibility by freezing water in dice

when they invent 'no' i will be excluded in its meaning

i am the political correspondent for unredeemed fate

of 8 children there will be no children

i cannot answer whole questions today

i don't want to disturb these zeroes in their nest

i will be unpopular if i arrest the moon

brother Ernst died of his own name in this place in 1916

i am not scared to assemble a death for others to use

unfound on a map brother Hermann killed himself in 1919

they wouldn't let me replace the idea of marriage with a 3yr old girl

until they dispense with the singular i will not be alive

i might answer half questions tomorrow

light succumbs to its finality at its birth

i calculate the number of exit signs that have never been read

i never wanted to hold a hand for this reason

i am not scared to assemble others for death to use

i have managed to reverse the age of this stone on the floor

as sometimes happens i was named after a dead brother

unless i'm by myself but not with myself i won't leave myself

as sometimes happens i was orphaned at 8

the doctor told me i was allergic to circles

i am so persuasive i can force a tumour to confess

of my peers i was the first to notice the bones in fruit

i taught that spider the value of a square web

i share what i don't have

i eat disrepair from this unimagined circle

with myself is the unself that has no self

i still want to make boats out of their skin

i've hung up so many memories the g in ago is broken

i hold the empty space in my head under the water in my head

i offer regret to optimism

twice i had to unlock their violence with their faces

with a swollen ankle my mind limps to the end of this thought

to wake up each morning i disguise my eyelids as splinters

in this fragment unity defends itself against the whole

i call forth any god imaginable with my paper trumpet

i turn my endings into earjuice

i lend money to my thoughts but they never pay me back

i have a 5'9" ampersand for company

as i hear i notate this firing squad of musical instruments

at every stage the actor must be every stage

i wear my pants this high to promote fabric architecture

finally my ego has written me a note and left me

i fetch voices out of their obedient slander

i won't divulge the reason to save the excuse

the bell will remove its dress every hour

repetition in a sentence sentences words to repetition

my paper trumpet improvises the protoprayer-jazz of saints

the bell kindly insists that i am still here

the rain is just my blood subtracted from its colour

when i am alone this is the apology i am not made of

uncolour is the silence i request

to penetrate a leaf i turn a page

i am the colour of silence

saliva is the code word for ink

i assassinate colour with grace

loss will be the new punctuation

i sleep to damage what is safe

i sleep to become a witness

my fingers cannot be asleep if i am my fingers

'the head lies in state with its lies' - a mortician's maxim

i wander inside the outside of every cage

i remember one phrase that gave me its blanket

i own the geology of every comma

i am covered in what should be covered in

these engines i throw at my ignition

they gave me a bag of grey hair for my birthday

i regret the presence of my feet

i decide to frighten my absence with a cough

my legs when measured against the tusks of a walrus are the same size

i give permission to the weather

i will spare the giant the giant's revenge

i invoice myself for my transgressions

with two elbows in each arm i make steps for my pulse

failure is the only primate without thumbs

i reject the presence of my hands

i would never open an envelope addressed to influence

lips other than mine have no access to satisfaction

everything that is finished i want to unfinish and leave unleft

i care for a bruise the way i care for a child

i threaten nothing with its curious and sacred potential

i am not as unusual as myself

the buttons on my shirt seem arrogant

who would make a child into a bruise to be cared for

sister Fani has a mother-of-pearl forehead

i am the stowaway in a pregnancy older than retaliation

stillness is envy still sipped until still

with stones in pockets my father purchased an accelerated end

lips frequently misread their triumph over form

i never intend to keep my appointment with doubt

i saw a horse sleeping in another man's hand

i have demanded that the bell put its dress back on

stillness can be sipped but still not protected

i herd the artificial lambs through my gospels

strange that doubt had no holes in its socks

if my own hero defeats my own army who will bury the dead

what is left of this description goes on describing itself

i could bring down the Swiss government with my good health

i did not walk this far to come this far

it is not abnormal to beat your saliva with a whisk

i have my skin take every third Sunday off

i offer the snake the use of my hands

my walking conjures the rhythm of my mother's pulse

these marches carry my brain above itself/itself a throne marching

how far could two men stretch a noun in 35 years

which hand would the snake become if it had a choice

by moving at this pace i warp their achievements

music unsettles a vacancy deep within sound procreation

i re-ask the emblem if it can re-cite its praise

i shun the vision until it sees me

this flight will overdose on birds

i have decided to add East & West poles to this earth's configuration

what is it that grazes over me when i lie down

the way i travel is to feed walls to distance

i don't believe light should be allowed inside cameras

i hallucinate the bird into thinking i can fly

i re-quest each vision to coarsely re-enact its objective necessity

105

i tend the damp majestic forest by cutting triangles into bark

there is nothing as sudden as what never happened

the supply of snails i need for my work i breed in my mouth

i believe thunder is the casualty in someone else's argument

the supply of snails i nourish with this plug of tobacco in my cheek

because he's dead i wish i'd sent that Glarner Birnbrot recipe to Lenin

this butterfly can't talk with its colour full

naturally i keep a tally of every breath except the last one

this insinuating maths offers me everything but maybe

in a couple of million years i'll be a couple of hours old

they give me a new pencil every week

my one pencil i sharpen with the glare on the window sill

this Sütterlin script i bind through a mound of words 10' high

this Sütterlin script i cross-hatch as Mikrogramme onto spored memory

i am not among the tame and yet no wild animal*

**i was myself the one who spoke to me

i myself am as tall as a clock

106

i put my shoes on the bed and myself on the floor

i situate myself beneath the physics of my fingerprint

i am not here i am not where i am

i leak emergencies onto paper

all i want for Christmas is a heart-attack with legs

my masks sobered with worn eternity

i am about to think of something that will make art redundant

† The writer Robert Walser (1878-1956) and the artist/writer Adolf Wölfli (1864-1930) were both patients at the Waldau Mental Asylum. Their occupancies overlapped in the years 1929-1930.

* Wölfli. A. *The Cradle to The Grave*, (trans. A. Shields). *The Art of Adolf Wölfli*, New Jersey, Princeton University Press, 2003.

** Walser. R. *She addressed me in the formal style.* (trans. C. Middleton). *Speaking to the Rose*, Lincoln, University of Nebraska Press, 2005.

Notes

opening epigraph

From the poem *Tre Alberi di Gelso* (Three Mulberry Trees) by Giordano Pastore; (*Poesie Scelte* - Badia a Elmi Editore, 2013). Translation Simone Gelli.

sectional epigraphs 1.,2.,3.

The words 'forward or backward', 'to the side', and 'feet together' taken from https://www.dancing4beginners.com/waltz/#steps

the unconsumed apple

In 1925 Oppenheimer left a poison apple on the desk of his tutor Patrick Blackett at Cambridge University.

James Stirling is pulled into a flat line

In 1992 architect James Stirling died during a routine operation due to the over-administration of anaesthetic.

propeller / Le Corbusier

In 1938 Le Corbusier was involved in an accident while swimming. His leg was severely cut by a power boat propeller.

explaining pictures to a dead hare

Based on a photograph by Ute Klophaus from the performance piece of the same name by Joseph Beuys (1965).

notes taken by a doll in Vienna

OK = Oskar Kokoschka + AM = Alma Mahler.

AM /OK is based on Kokoschka's chalk drawing *Alma Mahler Spinning Kokoschka's Intestines*, 1913. Alma Mahler had a pregnancy terminated during their relationship. Kokoschka explored this theme in several prints and drawings. **OK /AM** is based on Kokoschka's lithograph *A Male and a Female Strangle a Snake*, 1914 from the series *Allos Makar*. Following the breakup of their relationship Kokoschka had a life size doll made of Alma.

corduroy linesman

Written as part of a remix project for Cordite: Creative Commons – The Remixes (33.1). The poem used was *Flarfing Ginsberg* by Pascalle Burton.

the stones are turning

The line *as at a cup my life-blood seemed to sip* is from Coleridge's *The Rime of the Ancient Mariner*.

SPLICE

Written for *The Poetry Picture Show*, a collaborative film and poetry project commissioned by Johanna Featherstone at the Red Room Company (Sydney).

Acknowledgements

The poems in *axolotl waltz* were written on Gubbi Gubbi land. I acknowledge original inhabitants and the spiritual and creative significance of that region. I also thank the super-geo beings that are the Glasshouse Mountains for allowing me to sit in on their chess game for a split second.

Many thanks to family and friends who formed the thoughts, memories, and conversations in and around these works: Gordon, Noela, Ariel, Isaak, Kym, Luke, Kathryn, Sandra, Simone, Josie, Ian W, Craig, Fiona, Peter, Susan, Colleen, Karen, Shane, Anita, Laurelle, Graham, Fay, Ian N, Caeleigh, Bruce, Katherine, Hamish, Helen, Margie, Richard, Tom S, Felicity, Bronwyn, Nina, George, Victoria, Steve, Margot, Brett, Jim, Shirley, Stephen, Gina, Graeme, Laurie, Isma, John, Nona, Pascalle, Ian P, Charlie, Teresa, Matthew, Karen, Gil, Lici, Elizabeth, Rob, Rebecca, Grant, David M, David P, Judy, David B, Sheridan, Angela, Kerry, Joe, Dai Li, Lawrie, Leighton, Patrida, Stuart, Tom B, Sandra, Jon, Josh, Jamie, Peter, Noreen, Sean, Bo, Eugene, Matt, Rowan, Graham N, Julie, David S, Marian, Madonna, Davida and Alun.

I'd also like to single out Tony Frazer at Shearsman for being the first to sublet a rectangular room to a number of these poems.

Thank you to Tiffany Johnson as logistic and aesthetic mentor in all things book publication.

Thank you to Arryn Snowball for the cover image plus the bales of suffused simpatico.

And both hand-knitted and pre-fab thanks to David Musgrave, Morgan Arnett, and Ross Gillett at Puncher & Wattmann for tossing you the keys to allow you to open this page.

faces back in the pack of the weary croupier.

Some works in this collection were previously published in *Australian Book Review, Best Australian Poems 2008, Australian Poetry Journal, Cordite, foam:e, The Poetry Picture Show* (Red Room Company), *Queenslanders All Over, Shearsman* (UK), *time with the sky* (Newcastle Poetry Prize Anthology 2010).

www.ingramcontent.com/pod-product-compliance
Lightning Source LLC
Chambersburg PA
CBHW030847090426
42737CB00009B/1131